SELF HELP

The Destructive Ego

*Recognize and Tame
the Enemy Within*

By: Fred Mercado

Table of Contents

Introduction

I want to thank you and congratulate you for downloading the book, *"SELF HELP: The Destructive Ego, Help Tame and Control the Enemy Within"*.

This book contains proven steps and strategies on how to identify which ways your ego is harming you in life and take control back. We will go over multiple areas of your life that could use improvement and simple, easy to understand ways to fix them. Many people are going through life struggling unnecessarily, all because they don't realize what the ego is, how to recognize it, and how to get it under control.

Here are Some Signs that you need to Work on your Ego:

Almost everyone can improve their ego, but how do you know for sure if you fall under this category? Let's look at a few signs:

- **No Accomplishment Ever Keeps you Satisfied for Long:**

You work and work toward a goal, telling yourself that once you reach it, you will be happy and fulfilled. The problem is that once you do, you still feel unhappy.

- **You are Constantly feeling Insecure or Envious:**

You need to compare yourself to others ceaselessly in order to find satisfaction. You don't feel okay with where you're at unless you can see that it's better than where someone else is. You gain happiness from feeling smarter or better than others.

- **You have Many Burned Bridges in your Past:**

Perhaps this is a long series of bad breakups, or friendships that fell by the wayside after a big argument. Typically, it's a sign that your ego is out of control if you have trouble keeping healthy relationships.

- **You have a lot of Addictions, even to Socially Acceptable Things like Coffee or Social Media:**

Ego thrives on constantly needing something, and this can take many forms. If you find that you are always reaching for something, it's likely a sign that your ego needs some work.

If you found yourself nodding or mentally agreeing with one or more of these points, you need to work on your ego. The good news is, it's easy to fix and just takes commitment. If you're ready to improve your life, relationships, and sense of self, this book is perfect for you!

How to Take Back Your Personal Power:

Our ego makes us feel as though we're never good enough, creates strong emotional reactions in us that make us feel powerless, and then forces us to take the blame. This is not our natural state of being, which is why it's so hard to recognize and control. However, fixing this is perfectly possible and starts with knowledge and your own mindset on the matter.

The quality of life all begins with your mentality and beliefs. A person with a healthy relationship with their ego and a positive mentality will prosper and enjoy life, while a person who lives under the rule of their ego will suffer and act out a number of unhealthy behaviors, usually without even realizing why they keep sabotaging themselves and ruining opportunities. The good news is, you don't have to keep doing this.

If you would like to conquer addictions, improve relationships, and become the best version of yourself, you've come to the right place. I will walk you, step by step, through proven methods for conquering your ego and becoming the best you possible. This book is valuable to both men and women, and will show you how to have a successful career, love life, and general existence.

Thanks again for downloading this book, I hope you enjoy it!

Please visit me on my website at The New Leaders

www.thenewleaders.com

Chapter 1: What is the Ego?

The ego is an idea of self that we have created. We are an "intelligent person" or a "bad speller". We are "great at sports" or "awkward and ungraceful". We observe ourselves and go through many experiences in life and then construct the stories about ourselves which we will live by. Even when evidence that may contradict one of our ideas of self comes up, we don't even notice it. This is how strongly we are attached to our ego, or idea of self.

How to Tell What Your Ego Looks Like:

- To figure out what your ego is, take a look at all of your beliefs about who you are, what your personality consists of, and your abilities and talents.

- You can do this by writing down a list of all of your qualities and personality traits, such as "shy", "outgoing", or "talkative".

- You can even make a list of things you're good at, things you're bad at, or characteristics that you see as unchangeable about yourself or life. Make three lists with a category for each.

Writing these down will give you a clear picture of what your personal ego looks like, but keep in mind that it is far more complex than this and that some parts of it will remain hidden to you.

You believe that you simply "are" certain ways, and see this as a static and unchanging thing, which stays constant. These ideas of who we are will be based around true qualities of ourselves, but the actual mental idea of that self may not be as real as you imagine. What if you found out that these ideas don't have to be true? Are you skeptical? Let's look deeper into this and find out.

Your "Unchangeable" and "Permanent" Characteristics:

It may seem as though these are unchangeable facts to come to terms with. I mean, you've proved time and time again that you're intelligent in one way, but dumb in others. You have shown over and over that you are clumsy, just look at how often you trip over your own feet! But what if some parts of you are only true because you believe them to be? What if your expectations of "how you are" are the main factor in creating your personality?

Let's look at some of the ways we can recognize the ego and thus free ourselves from it more and more.

Our Mental Relationship with the Ego:

In reality, these factors of ourselves and our reaction to them are a dynamic and active part of who we are, but far from the whole picture. Our attachment to this mental image of our personalities causes a lot of unnecessary drama and suffering in our lives, especially when what we believe and what we observe are in disharmony. The ego likes to hide behind the words "me" and "I" in all of these thoughts we have about ourselves, gaining a sense of comfort from "knowing" what the facts are and what to expect.

Each time we engage in one of these thoughts, such as "I am ugly", and go along with the thought even slightly, believing that it tells a true story about us, we reinforce the ego. These thoughts first start appearing in our minds when we are just children, and arise from events in life such as being picked on at school or being praised or punished by our parents or teachers. In every part of the world, developing an idea of self is a common part of becoming socialized.

You've probably heard the word "ego" plenty of times to describe a variety of phenomena. Why is this word so hard to describe or define? It's because it is not one thing, specifically. The ego consists, in reality, of countless complex beliefs that have been acquired over a person's entire life. With years and years of information and experiences being used to build this construction, it makes sense that these beliefs are widely varied and may even contradict each other at times.

The Difficulty of Noticing What is You vs Ego:

To make this even more complicated, the ego of each individual is completely different. Just because one person figures out a way to describe and identify all the separate portions of their ego (which may be impossible, to begin with), it wouldn't necessarily give a good indication of what yours is like, because we're all so different.

The difficulty is realizing what your own ego is like is even harder when you take into consideration that the modern West world doesn't necessarily condone or encourage looking inside ourselves to notice stuff like this. But the good news is, it's up to us whether we want to commit to this path and become stronger people who are free from our ego. It isn't possible or reasonable to want to eliminate the ego completely, but we can come a long way with a bit of dedication and awareness.

How to Recognize your Ego:

The ego can be hard to spot since it hides behind seemingly true opinions, descriptions of ourselves that we are attached to, and also because we aren't used to paying attention to it. You can get an idea of it by paying attention to specific thoughts, similar to the examples given at the beginning of the chapter. Any thought that has to do with "I" or "me" can give you some insight into what your ego looks like.

Examples of Ego-based Thoughts:

"This always happens to me."
"Why can't I ever do anything right?"

"I am always late for everything."
"I look better than her today."
"My freckles make me look ugly."
"That person is way better looking than me."

You probably noticed that each of these thoughts is centered on yourself and tends to represent a victim mentality or very fatalistic thought. Ego centered thoughts are always about the self and typically make extreme, absolute statements about the nature of your personality, hinting at the fact that they cannot be changed. They tend to have a feeling tied to them, though they don't always have this.

But the simplest way to recognize what an ego thought is, is by noticing the strong emotional reactions left behind by it. Feeling frustrated with a close friend, insecure thoughts, needing to be right all the time, jealous feelings you can't explain, the need to be impressive, and more are all the result of your ego. At first, you may find it simpler to recognize the symptoms of drama and the emotions that happen as a result, rather than the actual ego that causes them.

The Strong Emotional Basis of Ego-Based Thoughts:

A difficult aspect of our ego is the fact that it creates strong emotional charges and then shifts the blame to us for how these charges make us feel. The frustration and anger we feel in response to this is stirred up by false beliefs created by the ego, often fueled by the need to be right and know better than another person. This phenomenon also tends to go hand in hand with a victim mentality of injustice or feelings of betrayal. Once we react strongly with frustration, we may feel guilty for our expressions of the emotions.

This is when the ego decides to shift into a mode of knowing better or feeling righteous and then berating us for our overreactions. This creates a nasty cycle of bad feelings and guilt, often leading to dysfunctional habits and unhealthy relationship patterns. Even as it has these thoughts, the ego tends to take on the identity of feeling like the "dumb person" or "idiot" who wasn't smart enough to know better and deserves intense blame or even hatred for the overreactions.

All of these complex reactions, beliefs, and attitudes occur in your mind, and although they aren't a natural part of us at all, we believe that they come directly from us. However, if this were true, and these were genuine expressions coming from our deepest selves, they wouldn't be so contradictory, and we would be perfectly capable of controlling or putting a stop to them.

The Difference between the Ego and You:

To someone who is not aware, it can be hard to decipher what is their real, authentic self and what is the ego. Often times, they look back at the way they handled an emotional situation and have to ask themselves what took over them and made them act certain ways. Even after they have calmed down and logically analyzed the experience, they don't have the consideration to realize which pieces of their mentality works as something separate from their true self.

The Cycle of Self-Blame and Condescension:

This brings about a situation where every emotional reaction they have, they blame themselves for using one of the condescending mental voices they have. Essentially, they are being hijacked by the ego, which takes over the self-analysis and transforms it into a process of blame and harsh criticism of the self.

When a person's ego doesn't have the ability to process things in a constructive, self-reflecting way, it's impossible for you to see the basis of your emotional turmoil and drama, since your ego is always reaffirming its own existence and cowers behind the self-blame and harsh criticisms. This can lead to a lot of dysfunction, which we will cover later in this book.

Chapter 2: How does it Control You?

The ego is not an inherently bad thing, and actually helps us a lot with interacting with the world, ourselves, and others. Developing an ego is a healthy thing to do, and only becomes a problem when the idea of self is wrong, negative, or even too confident. Considering the fact that we begin creating this idea of self as kids, it only makes sense that it may not be entirely accurate as we grow older.

A Healthy Mental Habit Gone Wrong:

The problem begins when the mechanism grows to a point where it's not under our control anymore and instead ends up running us. What first was created as a protective measure, meant to strengthen our sense of healthy identity, has now turned into a nasty monster that appears to want to sabotage us.

It's important to realize that the ego does not necessarily have bad intentions or want to sabotage us, however much it may seem that way. It is an entity, and like any other living entity, only wants to survive. The ego feeds off of drama and strong emotions, so each time you feed it this stuff, it gets stronger and realizes that this is what is necessary to sustain its existence. It then creates more of this, however it can.

The Nature of the Ego:

Usually, people use the term "ego" in a way that is associated with being arrogant or thinking one is above other people. But this simplified definition is not the whole picture, and arrogance is only one small portion of what the ego is. Actually it's entirely possible to possess both a positive self-image and a negative one at the same time and only be aware of the contradictions at certain times. The bad beliefs we hold about ourselves create our negative self-image, while the good beliefs make up our positive self-image. In combination, these two groups of beliefs form the ego.

It isn't uncommon that these two sides of us balance each other out and are equally strong. People who tend to be really tough on themselves about their negative self-image may suffer from constant and intrusive thoughts of being worthless or not good enough. This can be a harsh feeling to withstand, and to try to deal with the harsh feelings, they may try to mask them with overcompensation, trying to come across as very confident and secure in themselves, while simultaneously battling emotions of inadequacy, insecurity, and worthlessness.

11

Confidence vs the Ego's Arrogance:

The confidence that arises from a healthy assessment of the self is completely different than arrogance. Someone can be perfectly confident about their own skills or abilities, accepting themselves completely, without becoming arrogant in personal interactions with other people.

Humility and modesty often get mistaken for other traits like insecurity or shyness, but someone who has true modesty is truly at peace and present through all that may come in life and their own selves. Being confident without being arrogant, having modesty without being shy, those are true manners of a well-adjusted personality that isn't fraught with the issues of an unhealthy ego.

Is the Ego a Necessary Evil?

A lot of people would assume that the ego is not necessarily inherently bad. These same people would say that the ego is necessary to succeed. The idea of succeeding, in this example, would mean winning status, honor, and attaining material possessions or prestige. It is only when your ego is gigantic that you will be able to succeed in particular job paths or get to the top of the chain. For example, in jobs where harming others is necessary, reaching the top would mean sacrificing your respect of other humans for the sake of serving your ego.

Ideally, your paths in life will not go against your better judgment or require that you sacrifice your spiritual health in favor of them. Your profession should align with your truest self and conscience; only then can you be healthy mentally and have a ego that is not harmful. If you find that your job or relationship can only succeed if you nurture a harmful or selfish ego, you should probably not continue along that path, or pursue that path in a different way.

The Inner-critic within Us All:

The ego controls you by constantly making you feel like you can't be good enough. Have you ever accomplished something great, only to have the pleasure and satisfaction wear off within minutes? This is because the ego will always ask more of you, no matter how well you've done. It only takes a small comment from an unsuspecting person, someone cutting you off in traffic, or a sad story on TV to upset your entire mood, even if you had woken up feeling great that day.

The false you (the ego) thrives on drama and thoughts of injustice. The victim mentality is at the foundation of the ego, and it cannot survive without this. This is how it keeps you under its control, and you will stay its slave until you start to notice the effect it has on you and find ways to reverse it.

The good news is, once you become aware of it, half the battle is over. Staying conscious about the ego is the number one most important factor in all of this. So, how do you lessen the ego and become a healthier person? Let's find out in the next chapter.

Chapter 3: Habits that Lessen Ego

Since your ego is complex and multi-leveled, it is not effective or practical to seek to get rid of it all at the same time, and it's not likely that you could conceivably do that. Similar to a huge bush or tree that has grown out of control in your backyard, you can't just throw it out or pull it out of the ground at will. Instead, you lop off pieces in manageable chunks, one at a time.

Having Realistic Expectations for Ego Goals:

Don't expect this to happen instantly, or you will only cause yourself unnecessary heartache trying to fight it. Instead, commit to getting better and better, each day, in small chunks at a time. As long as you are moving forward each day, you're doing great.

You can view the process of getting rid of fake beliefs and poisonous mental habits in the same way as removing a burdensome tree from the garden. You start with identifying thoughts separately that exist to strengthen the ego, detaching from them, then eventually get to a place where you can let them go, seeing yourself as separate from the fake identify put forth by your ego.

Meditation:

Perhaps hailed as the number-one method for noticing your ego and separating yourself from it, meditation is a great way to detach from ego habits. Religious sects sing the praises of meditation frequently, and for good reason, since it pays off immensely to those who commit.

• Noticing your Thoughts:

Meditation, contrary to popular belief and rumor, isn't about trying to stop thinking. It's about learning to notice your thoughts. Once you begin to do this, you will notice that most of the thoughts that cross your mind throughout the day seem to come out of nowhere and many of them don't even make sense.

• The Constant Stream of Nonsense:

We don't choose our thoughts, which is why advertising is a successful business. We are subjected to hundreds of things each day, often against our will, and this is especially through in the era of social media. How many times per day do you find yourself thinking of some random nonsense that you saw earlier and don't care about at all? The good news is that you don't have to be subjected to this.

- **Disengaging from Worthless Thoughts:**

As I said earlier, the idea is not to *stop* these thoughts from occurring, but to notice them when they appear, and to learn the art of selecting which thoughts are worthy of focus. A stream of thought in any given person's head will typically look like this, "I need to buy milk, what was she wearing, he said that earlier, how about tomorrow, those jeans..." It is literally a chaotic jumble. When you learn to meditate, you can watch this stream of thoughts float by in your mind and ignore the ones that aren't worth focusing on.

- **Choosing Empowering Thoughts:**

Out of all of those random and crazy thoughts that pass through your brain at any given moment, there are some that are worthwhile, and those are the healthy, positive thoughts. When you learn to disengage from this endless stream of thoughts, you acquire the gift of selective focus.

The average person is tossed around all day long by this cascade of thoughts, and meditation gives you back the power to be the one in control. You will start to recognize when your ego starts to try to take over, and you will be giving yourself the option of saying no.

Finding a Creative Pursuit:

Creativity is a great source of inspiration that can disengage you from the constant chatter of your ego. People often believe that they are "not creative", but this isn't true. Every person is creative, and the only thing holding you back from believing this, is your ego. Taking up a creative pursuit will:

- **Find Meaning and Worth Outside of Possessions:**

Following your creative calling is about getting in touch with your intuition and free-flowing spiritual side. This part of you doesn't care about prestige and glory or how much money you have in the bank. The point of this side is expression and genuine passion. Creating something beautiful with your pursuit is only a bonus and the true joy comes from the act of creation.

- **Become More Confident, not Cocky:**

As mentioned earlier, the ego thrives on arrogance, not true, healthy self-esteem. When you know that you can create something from your soul, your sense of self grows in an abundant and valuable way, rather than a superficial one. This will make you more comfortable with your genuine self and make your spirit grow immensely. You can then inspire others and help them shine their light.

- **Calming and Soothing your Mind:**

A huge part of getting caught up in ego thoughts is being stressed out, and creativity is the best way to disengage from this and relax, finding your center. If you find that you're being taken over by anxious ramblings of the mind, a perfect way to separate yourself from this and get free is to pick up an artistic activity such as painting, drawing, or writing. Writing is especially valuable because it makes the thoughts that are ego appear clearly and helps you to separate yourself from them, making them lose their power over you.

Walking Outside in Nature:

Humans in modern day live in an unnatural environment and rarely see the outdoors. This leads to a lot of discomfort that we often don't even realize. To neutralize the ego and become healthier individuals, we must regain contact with our roots as members of this planet and start going outside more. Going outside will:

- **Get you in Touch with your Inner, True Self:**

Being outside immediately stills the rabid voice in our heads, which means that we have a chance to hear the small voice that represents our true self. Nature is our original home, as humans, so something about our minds recognizes this fact. Seeing nature doing its thing naturally can help to inspire us to learn to accept ourselves, shortcomings and all.

- **Help you see Beyond Conditioned Thoughts:**

As mentioned earlier, spending more time outdoors will help you hear the small voice of your true self, which will make all of the false thoughts seem less powerful and more alien. All they are is conditioned responses that don't have to be listened to. When you find your strength that comes from within, these thoughts have no chance to take over your mind and control you. You have your power back.

- **Calm your Mind and Help you Disengage from Ego:**

When we walk outside to enjoy the fresh air and see greenery around us, it calms our mind. Studies have shown that work days are more successful when someone can have a view of a tree outside of their window, which proves the effect nature has on us. We can only choose to say no to the ego when we recognize it for what it is. This requires spending more time doing calming activities that are simple and quiet, to put us in touch with what's going on in our heads. Regularly taking walks in nature will be a great help in this pursuit.

Hanging out with Children:

Children have less developed egos, so they are truer and more themselves, something many adults have forgotten. Hanging out with them can really help you to begin thinking in a clearer and simpler way.

- **Become Inspired:**

It can be inspiring to be around people who are much younger than us and still have a very pure spirit about them that isn't yet bogged down with ego. Many children are caring and not as self-conscious as adults, which means we have a lot we can learn from them. We have a habit of assuming that kids don't know as much as adult, but perhaps they realize things that we have simply forgotten.

They also provide unfiltered insight that can be inspiring, since the average adult in the West world tends to be very stifled and afraid to express their true selves. To be around people who express their true selves can help us develop the same bravery. This can free you from the ego.

- **Get in Touch with your Creative Self:**

Kids are creative in the unabashed way that adults often forget how to be. Since doing more creative activities can be so helpful for disengaging from the ego, it makes sense that being around children could help with this. You could volunteer or begin a job at a daycare center, or if you already have kids, make a point to spend more time with them and see what you can learn from them.

- **Learn how to be More Playful with Life:**

The ego likes to make us believe that life is one big, serious drama. This is the opposite of how the natural spirit is. To a well-balanced and healthy person, and to many children, life is about taking events lightly and enjoying play. Children eventually become dramatic and serious only as they get conditioned to be that way, from adults with egos.

We can look to children who still have their sense of wonder and joy and learn great lessons from them. This may even teach you to view the antics of your ego in a positive, humorous light, instead of getting discouraged by them.

Getting Rid of some Possessions:

Owning a lot of stuff is not an inherently bad thing, but it can start to weigh on you, bog you down, and intensify your ego. It's too easy to start equating your own sense of worth with what you own, when you have a lot of stuff. You start becoming afraid of what would happen if you didn't have it. In other words, your ego fears that it would cease to exist without the material possessions.

- **Make you Less Worried about Material Things:**

Getting rid of a lot of stuff will instantly make you feel lighter. You won't have to constantly worry about taking care of your possessions and you will discover a sense of self that is not tied up in the material realm. Since living free from ego requires being in touch with your still, inner-voice, it can help, for some people, to have less stuff. Your spirit can be free instead of bogged down by material items.

- **Help you Enjoy Giving to Others:**

At first, when you think about getting rid of specific items, you will feel serious resistance. But if you push through this feeling and get rid of it anyway, especially when you're giving it to a friend, you will experience a serious sense of freedom.

We are all so attached to physical items without even realizing it and this is a great way to get free from that addiction. Try having a yard sale, giving to good will, or having your friends come over and take some things from your house. It may sound crazy, but I guarantee it will be life changing, if you have never done this before.

Starting a Journal:

This was mentioned briefly in the creativity section of this chapter, but it deserves its own section. You don't have to be a fantastic writer to start a journal, all you have to do is commit to the practice and make sure you write every day. If you don't know what to say at first, that's okay, just begin, and it will come to you with time. If you start a journal, you will:

- **Be able to Soothe your Own Mind:**

Instead of constantly looking outside of yourself for gratification or calm, you will develop the skill of being able to calm your mind yourself, by writing through your issues as they appear. When you write, you get in touch with the version of yourself that is not tied up in the ego. It's also easy to see your own mental patterns that hold you back and sabotage you.

- **Gain Valuable Insight into your Mental Patterns:**

When you keep up with writing in a journal consistently, you can't help but notice certain patterns in your own way of speaking with yourself, reflecting on thoughts, or saying certain things. Since the way we speak to ourselves has a lot to do with what type of person we become, this is something important to notice.

It's very easy to live day in and day out without ever knowing what our internal dialogue actually sounds like. We get so used to these constant conversations we have with ourselves that it just becomes background noise that we filter out. But it continues to run and affect everything about our day, so getting some insight into what it's like is a smart idea. You might learn that certain ways you communicate with yourself

25

are harmful and need to be dropped. Becoming aware of this will give you the freedom to start making changes to better yourself and talk to yourself in a respectful and healthy way.

- **See your Progress in Personal Development:**

We all have an idea of where we think we "should" be in life. Since we are constantly falling short by our own standards, it's easy to pass along through accomplishments and barely notice them. We achieve one goal and then instantly start looking for another one to take up our attention, not pausing to celebrate the victory we just had.

When you start a journal and go back to read old entries, the progress becomes clear and obvious. You can no longer ignore the great work you've done or how far you have come when you see how you used to be, compared to now. This can be extremely encouraging because it reminds you that, although I may not always feel like it, you are growing and progressing all the time.

Challenging Yourself:

To challenge yourself means to constantly grow and commit to bettering yourself all the time. This can be something that lessens the ego or at least helps you become more aware of it, since doing unfamiliar things is something the ego doesn't necessarily enjoy. If you make it a habit to challenge yourself every day, you will:

- **Learn Valuable Skills to Improve Yourself:**

When you know that you have real skills that offer value to others, you develop a sense of self that is genuine, instead of insecure. Arrogant or cocky people have a sense of lack because they fear that they don't have anything to offer. Truly self-assured people know that they have much to offer others, and for this reason, can stand confidently in themselves no matter where they are or what they are doing.

- **Get over the Fear of Looking Silly:**

When someone decides to try something new, they are rarely great at it, instantly. It takes time, effort, patience, commitment, and yes, a bit of looking silly, at first. Think about someone trying gymnastics who has never done it before, do you think they will look graceful and flexible? No, but the willingness to get out there and try regardless of how they look is what makes them become great, eventually.

Realizing that developing a skill or pursuing something *you* want regardless of how you will appear to others is a great way to strengthen your true self and lessen your ego.

Listening to Loved Ones:

The beauty of having people close to you that you trust is being able to share and listen to each other. Most people "listen" with the intention of waiting until the other person is done so they can talk. It takes effort and work to truly listen to another person and to be present for them in that very moment. Making sure you actually listen consciously to the loved ones around you will:

- **Teach you that it's not All about You:**

The ego loves to assume that you are the center of the universe. When you disengage from that habit of wanting to be the center of everything, you take the ego's power away and show it that other people are equally important and worth listening to. When you sit still and listen to another person, pay attention to the urge to

- **Strengthen the Bonds in your Life:**

Close loved ones are valuable sources of strength for us, especially when the relationship operates from a sense of real love instead of ego gratification. When you listen from the heart, the person you are with feels that and your bond becomes stronger, creating a mutual safe space for you and the person to be yourselves free from superficial ego wishes.

Learning to be a good listener will strengthen your true self and draw others to you, as well.

Becoming Physically Healthier:

Our society often forgets the strong tie between physical health and mental well-being. When we are constantly ingesting sugar and processed foods, it's no wonder that our minds are a mess and our stress levels are through the roof.

When you become healthier in a physical way, making sure you get plenty of exercise, drinking a lot of water, and paying attention to how you feed your body, you will discover that you become mentally healthier, as well. Becoming healthier will:

- **Help you see Value in Simple Joys:**

Exercising gets you back in touch with your body. We evolved to walk many miles a day and constantly be on the move. To be separate from this basic fact of life is to forget what it means to be human, which is why our egos have grown to enormous and unmanageable sizes.

Being more health-conscious will also teach you the art of eating for nourishment instead of stimulation, a simple and basic joy that we have also lost touch with. Learning to listen to the natural calls of your body and feed it with nutritious food will put you back in touch with the basic humanness we have lost in our modern world that is obsessed with convenience.

- **Encourage Others around you to Improve Themselves:**

The ego doesn't care much for helping others to succeed or be truly happy, unless it's for a selfish reason. By becoming healthier, you will inspire others to do the same, which is a selfless way to spread joy that is beyond the ego. Be an inspiring example to those around you by embodying health physically and mentally.

Committing to Recognizing and Improving your Ego:

The ego-based images of ourselves have been created over years and years of habit, emotions, and thoughts. We live inside of these selves and constantly reinforce them, without even realizing it. When we come to terms with the fact that we want to decipher who our genuine selves are in the midst of this fortress of habit, it's important to note that it won't happen overnight, or even over the course of multiple days.

The point of this journey is not a quick fix. Yes, this is going to take some time, and definitely some commitment, but it will be worth it. Think about any valuable skill you've developed over the course of life; walking, doing math, reading, writing.

How to be Patient with your Progress in Working on the Ego:

Anything that is valuable and worth doing will require commitment, lots of time, and plenty of faithful practice. So what better favor can you do your future self than committing to letting go of the very thing that is holding you back from living fully?

- **Recognize that it will Take Time:**

There is no quick fix for working on mental issues. Don't expect to wake up tomorrow morning a completely different person. This will be a long process with changes that happen gradually and a little at a time, but committing to inner-work is the most valuable pursuit you can ever undertake.

The ego wants to make everything seem like a dire, urgent, life or death matter. If you find that that is how you're approaching this whole thing mentally, your ego has snuck in to try to take over.

- **Set Reachable Goals:**

Instead of giving yourself huge goals like "banish the ego completely" or "lose 100 pounds in two months", try to give yourself small, reachable goals each day and week. You can start with simple intentions like having less negative thoughts, going outside more often, picking up a meditation habit, being more creative, or saying nice things to loved ones more often.

Achieving these small goals will strengthen your sense of identity in a healthy and positive way and show yourself that you are capable of doing whatever you set your mind to. Then, you can gradually increase the intensity of your goals.

- **Celebrate Progress:**

Don't get so caught up in achieving goals that you forget to stop and celebrate your accomplishments. Did you make it through an entire day without thinking negative thoughts about yourself or mentally berating your own efforts? That is worth recognition! Give yourself credit where credit is due. This doesn't have to be a huge deal, even a small mental pat on the back is enough.

- **Do Ego Challenges:**

A great way to take control of your ego is to give yourself challenges that separate you from it, such as committing to noticing each time your ego tries to pull you in a certain direction. Let's take an example of someone cutting you off in traffic. The event happens, and your ego chimes in wanting to get all upset about the injustice and that "idiot" who almost hit your car.

You can take this as a challenge to remain separate from this impulse to get upset and instead just notice the ego as something separate from yourself. If you keep doing this, eventually you will get better and better at it until it happens with little to no effort and becomes a permanent habit.

- **Keep Charts:**

A great way to stay on top of your ego and note your progress is to keep charts for each area that needs work. Perhaps you can have a chart for negative thoughts and positive thoughts and try to lessen the negative and amp up the positive. Things like this are a lot easier to keep track of when you have a physical representation of them.

- **Resist the Urge to Brag to Others about it:**

When you start seeing progress and getting all excited about how far you've come in dealing with your ego, you may notice that you want to share that progress with others. That urge is your sneaky ego trying to get back in and take over to strengthen its own image.

Instead of sharing the news with everyone about your progress and how great it is, resist this urge and do it for yourself. This is not about being better at beating your ego than other people, or being such an impressive person. Those thoughts defeat the whole purpose of this exercise. Keep your progress to yourself.

The Results of Committing to this Path:

All in all, it's important to be proud of yourself for committing to the path of lessening the ego and, consequently, becoming a better and stronger person. You will get to enjoy your own independence, peace of mind, and healthier relationships as a result.

Lessening your ego makes you a more inspiring person who everyone enjoys being around. We all know that type of person who can walk into a room and instantly lift everyone's mood just by being there. These are people who live from the genuine soul instead of from the ego's insecure clinging. Getting on top of your ego and regaining your own personal power will make you a better friend, spouse, parent, and person, in general.

Living from the True Self vs Living from the Ego:

When we do things from ego, they are done with a selfish air to them that is inherently weak and insecure, but when we do things from our spirit, it shines through and we can have a great impact on the world around us. A lot of this starts with the relationships we have around us. In the next chapter, we will cover the ways that the ego can sabotage personal relationships and how to get around this and take back the reigns of connection.

Chapter 4: Improving Relationships

Ego definitely plays a large role in turning relationships sour, and this applies to family ties, friendships, and love arrangements. Your ego can destroy friendships that have been built up over years, and place huge wedges between blood ties, as well. If you look to your past and notice that you have patterns of failed relationships, it's time to consider that your ego might be involved in this.

The Difference between Self-esteem and Ego:

You hear the term "ego" typically used in tandem with negative qualities, but having a lot of self-esteem is considered a good thing. So, where is the line between the two? A person with a huge ego determines their own worth by material or external things, such as feedback from other people or how much money they have. When someone has a high sense of self-worth, they base their own esteem on their internal compass which reads beliefs, passions, or inspiring personal visions.

When someone has a huge ego, they are usually insecure and seeking to hide this in any way possible. Often these methods of hiding take shape as trying to appear as better than other people or seem highly important. This doesn't work so well with love relationships, since these partnerships tend to draw out our insecurities and have a way of forcing us to come to terms with them.

How Ego Makes Love Relationships Challenging:

We all have things we need to work on, but the ego hates to admit that. This means that when a partner points out an issue they have with us, our ego immediately goes into defense mode. Here are some examples of thoughts you may have in your relationship issues that are your ego:

- **How dare she say that to me?**

The ego thrives on injustice and goes into defensive mode as soon as it feels attacked. If you notice that you get angry easily when someone makes a comment to you and find yourself feeling justified in your overreaction, it's time to take a step back and realize that the ego is trying to take over.

He is just judging me right now:

This is a thought that seeks to draw attention away from a quality about yourself that could use some work or improvement. The ego hates to notice that it is not perfect, so instead of truly reflecting on feedback from loved ones, it prefers to blame the other and feel judged. This creates a convenient defense mechanism against having to face unpleasant truths about itself.

- **After all I do for them, this is what I get?**

The ego always wants to feel like it's the one doing all the good and getting blame all the time. This keeps it in a safe place where it doesn't have to do any work or reflection and instead can safely assume the other person is the one in the wrong. Unfortunately, this doesn't make you happy and only keeps you in a cycle of strong and negative emotions.

- **I Should say Something Mean to get Them Back:**

When you find yourself getting the urge to lash out hurtfully to your loved one, this is your ego trying to regain its hold over you. Instead of succumbing to this urge, which will only make you and the other person feel much worse, take a breath and step back from the feelings.

The urge to say hurtful things comes from feeling insecure, and when you realize this, it's much easier to resist that strong pull to hurt others. Commit to not acting from your ego with your loved one and this will transform your entire relationship.

Are the Thoughts Justified and Rational, or Ego-based?

Now, in some situations, these thoughts may be justified, but if you tend to find yourself overreacting to small situations with intense emotions and thoughts like this, you might want to check on your ego.

It can be frustrating to admit when we need to work on certain personality traits, and since the ego's entire existence is tied up in these personality traits, it feels extremely threatened by any questioning of the patterns that exist. So, how can you tell the difference? Intuition can be a valuable indication. Are the words that the loved one is saying to you ringing true to you on a deep level, even if you might not want to admit it?

You are not your Personality Habits or Patterns:

There is a definite difference between who you are as a person and the mental habits you have developed over the course of life. A pattern of your mind can change without threatening your existence, and your personality remains, even if it's different. Since the ego mistakes your personality traits for *you*, any threat to those traits is taken as a direct attack and resisted with every force possible.

Someone can give you input on how to improve yourself or a certain quality of you and you can take it in a positive, beneficial way. You can become aware of your ego's tendency to want to close up, feel victimized, blame, and attack, and look beyond this reaction, knowing that you can ultimately grow from this interaction.

Staying Aware and Conscious to Grow from Relationships:

This is why it can be so painful when someone criticizes us. The ego tricks us into thinking it's a much bigger deal than it is. It's especially important to stay conscious of this in love relationships and to make sure that you can honestly assess the critiques your partner gives you and stay humble and open to improving.

That being said, there's a fine line between healthy critiques that can help you grow as a person and downright verbal abuse. If your partner is criticizing you to a point where it is extremely harmful and goes beyond just hurting your ego, that is an unhealthy situation that you should get out of.

People with huge egos don't love themselves and have no confidence, but the way they act outwardly can be deceptive. People who have a healthy level of self-love and self-esteem are assertive in a healthy way and confident in what they can do, are aware of their faults that need work, and accept and love themselves as they are.

The Commonly Known Definition of "Having an Ego":

Although we typically associate the meaning of having an ego with being arrogant or cocky, that's not necessarily the case. Every single person has an ego since it's necessary for survival. The ego lets us know that we are an entity separate from other things, and without this knowledge, we could not live. Regardless of the fact that we all have one, to be healthy and happy, we must learn how to keep our ego under our own control instead of letting it get out of hand and take us over. If your ego runs unchecked, you will suffer immense turmoil in every area of life, especially with your closest loved one.

Signs of Your Ego Trying to Take Over the Relationship:

When it comes to resentment, jealousy, fear, and anger, these are all products of your ego seeking to take control. Let's look more into a few signs that your ego is getting out of hand with close loved ones:

- **Holding onto an Unhealthy Arrangement:**

We have all seen that person who stays with the wrong partner because they are afraid to disengage from them. This could be out of fear of accepting that they judged their partner's character incorrectly, or the fear of being alone in general. Both of these are ego reactions. This happens a lot when people get abused or cheated on by a spouse or partner.

The ego becomes hurt and cannot accept the bad treatment we've received from our partner. It can't be reality that we have actually put all this work into the love and that it failed anyway. So we stay committed even when it harms us. To get free from a bad arrangement like this, a person must free themselves of their ego and attachment to the unhealthy situation.

- **Constant, Intrusive, Jealous Thinking:**

When your partner is enjoying a night out with their friends, do you constantly worry about what is going on? Fear-based jealousy from the ego can completely ruin a relationship. If you find yourself getting obsessed with those jealous thoughts that cross your mind, these will take over your relationship and cause you to hurt the other person, even if it's only in a subconscious way. Jealousy can make you believe all sorts of crazy thoughts and act in irrational ways.

This leads to fighting, blame, and even accusations sometimes. If this pattern continues, your partner will begin resenting the insecurity and eventually want to leave, all based on a fake story your ego fed to you and you believed.

- **Being Afraid of Getting Rejected:**

Feeling afraid of rejection is a natural human reaction to many things in life, and it doesn't have to be a problem, unless it gets out of control. If you find that you are shutting yourself down to new experiences or learning from fights in your relationship, your ego might be taking over.

If you notice that you are afraid to take chances out of fear of being rejected, that's your ego attempting to take over. It's important to stay conscious when this urge pops up and not to let it control your actions. Remember that fear of rejection is a natural part of being a human and that there isn't anything inherently wrong with the feeling. Let it come and then pass, otherwise you may ruin a relationship by letting it spin out of control.

- **Always Needing to be Right:**

For someone whose ego has a strong hold over them, being right can be the most important thing in the world. This is because the idea of rightness is tied up with having worth in life. They are trying to make up for a lack they feel inside by trying to seem smarter than their partner. This means that they cannot let go of an argument until they have won.

This urge can be so strong that everything else is lost at the expense of appearing right, including relationships with people at work, brothers or sisters, spouses or relatives. Eventually, you must come to terms with the fact that the fake satisfaction you get from winning arguments and always being right is not better than being truly happy and having healthy relationships.

How to Keep Ego from Ruining your Relationship:

Now that we've gone over some of the ways that ego tries to rear its head and sabotage our relationships, let's review some ways to keep this from happening. Following these steps will ensure that you take control over your own life and relationships and can have healthy, happy partnerships, or close bonds with family or friends:

- **Make a Habit of Writing about it:**

Any time you notice an ego habit making an attempt to take over your mind and ruin your emotions, write about it instead of lashing out. Record precisely what is making you feel jealous or insecure. After you do this, step away and do something else, whether it's going for a walk or getting some exercise.

After you have gotten to a calmer place, review your notes. You will be able to see the irrationality in the ego thoughts you wrote about. Perhaps you might find at times that you did have a justified reason to feel the way you did. Either way, writing will provide you with the necessary distance to process your emotions in a healthy way that is constructive instead of destructive to your relationship.

- **Talk to your Loved One about it:**

If you write about your emotions and find that you still feel insecure, jealous, or need to be write, talk to your partner or loved one about the feelings. Be sure to stay conscious, though, and keep your tone non-accusatory. Let your partner or loved one know what it is that bothered you and some suggestions for how you both can handle it better the next time around.

This can be a great chance to let your relationship get deeper, learn more about each other, and set some boundaries if necessary. If you reach out and share your true thoughts, you may find that you are surprised at how well it works to share.

- **Become Aware of your Own Insecure Thoughts:**

If you have a series of relationships behind you, you can look to these to find valuable insight into your own patterns of insecure thoughts. Where are these insecurities coming from? Have you been mistreated or cheated on by a past partner? This is a great chance to find out how your patterns developed and the best ways to prevent them from ruining your present relationship.

- **Be Completely Honest about Insecurities:**

We all have insecurities, and trying to pretend you don't does not help anyone, especially in relationships. You should sit

down with your partner and share the thoughts you have
scare you and make you insecure. Be sure to do this in a way
that does not attack or blame them, but instead speaks from
a genuine place.

- **Talk to your Friends about it:**

Friends can be a great source of strength when you get upset
about your partner. They can help you see which of your
thoughts may be based on the ego instead of reality. Don't be
afraid to open up to close friends to get some insight on your
own patterns and what needs work. The right friends can
give great advice and help you see things you may never have
seen otherwise.

Chapter 5: Constant Dissatisfaction

Have you ever been around someone who never seems to be satisfied, even when they appear to have received everything they claimed to want? This is someone who has a very strong ego, but all of us have this quality to some degree. The term "ego" aligns perfectly with the definition of a "false self", in other words, the picture of your own personality that you have made up, which you have come to mistakenly believe to be your unchangeable core.

The Ego Thinks It is Unchangeable:

You serve this entity as if its existence is objective and can never be changed, which is how it controls you. Some religions view this false self as the very center of ignorance, and that belief isn't far from the truth, since the core of our selves is ever-changing and cannot be defined in such simple terms. The ego is inherently simple and, consequently, quite foolish because it thinks that it has reality figured out. It clings to ideas of static definitions because it is insecure.

Humans are ever-changing entities with the power to be whatever they want (within reason, of course), but this is exactly what the ego fears you will discover. Many wise classes and religions have realized that the ego is the cause of almost all of the suffering and delusions of mankind.

How Your Ego is Making You Perpetually Dissatisfied:

Nothing is ever good enough for the ego, because it's a weak and constantly insecure being who cannot survive on calm, but instead thrives on fear. Once we become aware of how our ego is sabotaging different aspects of our lives, we can make conscious choices to be free from it. Here are the ways that your ego is making you unhappy, every day:

- **By Making you Compare Yourself with Others:**

The ego doesn't want to admit that other people might be more attractive, smarter, or better than us in any way. This will mean that the ego is constantly pointing out ways that you fall short in comparison to others. We are all different people with different strengths, so comparisons don't always make sense. It's important to remember this instead of feeling threatened when others shine.

- **By Putting Insecure Thoughts into your Head:**

Do you find that you obsess over insecurities? We all feel them, but if you discover that you have a hard time letting these natural thoughts go, your ego might be getting too strong and taking over. By pausing and noticing this tendency, you can disengage from this habit and take the power back from your ego.

- **By Thriving on Jealousy and Drama:**

The ego loves drama and jealousy or any feeling that makes it the victim. Wanting to hold onto jealousy or drama is not a habit of a healthy minded person, but is instead an indication that the ego is getting out of control. Jealousy is a natural emotion, but when it becomes obsessive, it's time to notice the way your ego is trying to sabotage you and put those thoughts to rest by recognizing them for what they are, ego drama.

- **By Keeping you Caught Up on Perceived Injustices:**

Life isn't always fair, but if you can't let go of injustices or situations that you felt victimized, that isn't healthy. When you notice that you are going off on a "poor me" tangent in your mind, that's the ego. You don't have to listen to those thoughts or let them take over. Instead, notice the thoughts as they occur with a calm and non-judgmental disposition. This will help you regain your own power and control over your mind and emotions.

How to Look Beyond the Constant Dissatisfaction of Ego:

When you serve your ego or let it run rampant without questioning, you are worshipping and strengthening a false identity. It can be compared to having amnesia and then making up a fake image for yourself to figure out who you are. When you stop to really consider it, it doesn't make much sense. So, how do we get rid of this? How do we learn how to be satisfied with life instead of constantly trying to escape from it?

- **Identify your Worth Outside of the External:**

What things about yourself make you feel good in a non-arrogant way? Perhaps you are good at being generous, a great listener to your friends, or a talented artist. If you can feel and notice these qualities about yourself in a way that isn't pompous or defensive, these are healthy qualities to focus on and gain satisfaction from away from the ego.

- **Get Rid of your Resistance:**

The very essence of the ego is resistance. Resisting the way you are, the way others are, your life situation, how much money you have, what you look like, etc. At a certain point, the best way to get beyond this constant dissatisfaction is just to let go of this resistance. It isn't a complicated process, although the ego loves to try to convince you that it is. It can be as simple as just deciding to drop a harmful thought that keeps popping up. It can be as easy as simply saying "no" the next time your ego is grasping for something.

- **Make a list of all of the qualities you value in yourself.**

Now that you have identified these qualities, make a list that you can look at whenever you are feeling like you aren't good enough. This gives you permission to decide your own worth outside of the constant whining of the ego. You are taking matters back into your own hands and deciding that you know what you are worth.

- **Start Noticing your Thoughts More Often:**

The ego can only take control of us and make us act irrationally if we don't notice the thoughts it generates. When you start listening to the thoughts in your head, this separates you from them enough for you to decide that you don't have to go along with everything that crosses your mind. Be sure to notice your thoughts in a way that is not judgmental, and this will take their power away, and help you regain control of your life and self.

- **Rediscover Simple Joys that feed the Soul:**

The ego has no interest in activities that don't strengthen its sense of identity, involve any drama, or stimulate the senses. For this reason, a lot of people find sitting in a room alone, walking quietly in the woods, or drawing to be very enjoyable. They are quiet activities that don't serve the false sense of identity.

However, when we're children, we find joy in simple pleasures. This is because our egos haven't fully developed yet and we still have the capacity to enjoy a wide variety of simple things. Rediscover this ability and you will take your power back. Even if it seems boring or under stimulating at first, stick with it and you will feel a new level of peace growing within you.

- **Pause and Reflect instead of Immediately Reacting:**

The ego's immediate desire is always to react instantly out of a strong emotion instead of pausing to calmly reflect, take a breath, and think it through. It's important to respond thoughtfully to life instead of always blindly reacting out of habit. This cycle can only stop when you decide to interrupt this habit cycle.

If necessary, take a walk and calm down before reacting to a situation in your life. This will help you see that getting upset and lashing out is not the best way to handle any situation.

Chapter 6: Being better at Work

Everyone strives to have a profession that will make them feel successful, and if this applies to you, it's a good idea to think through the reasons why you seek success. Is it the prestige that comes along with the job title you seek? Is it the money you will earn in that high profile position? Do you want to help others?

Some of your motivations for being better at your place of work could be centered on ego wishes. If you wish to approach work in a healthy, non-painful way that will benefit you and those around you and leave you happy and satisfied, here are some important things to think about.

<u>Can Certain forms of Competition be Harmful?</u>

Competition is not inherently a negative force, but can be problematic when compounded with certain job types that are centered on harming others or keeping them down. Take a look at your motivations for competing. Is it because you don't wish for others to succeed, or because your sense of self-worth is tied up in your image of yourself as a winner?

To Become Successful without Ego Attachment:

It's possible to be successful and move up at work without doing it for the wrong reasons or letting your ego take over. Here is how to be great at work without ego attachment:

- **Help Others Selflessly:**

The ego wants to steal all of the glory and look better than other employees to strengthen its false identity. Instead of letting this happen, fight the impulse by helping others at work. Perhaps a co-worker is behind on their work load, this is a perfect chance to step outside of your ego and offer them some help. Although letting them fail would make you look better and make your ego happy, being generous will bring you a sense of true satisfaction.

- **Get Involved in Extra Projects:**

A good way to make sure you're moving up at work for genuine reasons and not out of ego selfishness is to want to do more for the company without immediately thinking of how it will benefit you. Perhaps this would involve coming in early or staying late. It could be volunteering for projects that don't pay extra. You will find a sense of satisfaction that is beyond material gains or a big self-image.

- **Encourage Competitors:**

Are you hoping for a promotion that a co-worker just told you they are also hoping for? This is a good chance to offer them encouragement, instead of trying to sabotage them for your own gain. A truly healthy and confident person lifts people up because they are not selfish or threatened by the success of others. You could even go to your boss and tell them how great your co-worker has been doing at work during the week.

- **Find Extra Work that Doesn't Pay:**

This may sound crazy, but volunteering is a great way to move beyond ego and even improve your career by giving you the energy that comes from helping others selflessly. You could pick up a side job at the orphanage in town or even serve food at the homeless shelter on the weekends. Your ego will see no gain in this, but it's a great way to strengthen your genuine sense of well-being instead of catering to the false self-image.

- **Ask your Boss how you can Do Better:**

A great way to gain insight into your habits at work and become a stronger person is to humbly ask someone in a position above you how you can become a better employee and what you can work on. The ego doesn't like to admit that there are ways it can improve and that it is not, in fact, perfect, so asking questions like this allow you to step aside from the insecure clinging of the ego.

- **Use your Position of Power in a Selfless Way:**

If you find that you have been given a prestigious position at work, this could be a great chance to be a good boss and encourage others. Instead of succumbing to the urge to boss others around or use your new position to feel important, you can be a source of encouragement and strength to the workers below your position.

Ask them what they think on a situation at work instead of always assuming that you know best. When someone makes a mistake, take the time to pause and hear their side of the story instead of letting your ego take over and make you the one in the right. Being a boss is the perfect chance to practice not letting your ego control you. If you do this successfully, you will be a great boss who your employees look up to and respect.

Chapter 7: Ego and Addictions

We are all addicted to something. Our immediate association with the word addiction is usually that of a hopeless junkie begging in the streets, but many addictions are socially acceptable and thus virtually unnoticed and rationalized.

For example, some of us "have to have" our morning cup of coffee, which proves we're addicted to caffeine. Many of us, especially in the modern world, are glued to our electronic devices and almost constantly plugged into social media, hopelessly hooked on status updates without even realizing it. The ego loves having us addicted to something because it takes away our personal power and makes the ego stronger. The more dependent and weak we are, the stronger and more powerful the ego can become.

How the Ego is Tied Up in Addictions:

These may seem like two separate matters, but the fact is that the ego is inextricably entwined with additions. Addiction keeps us slaves to our impulses and takes our power away from us. Here is how your ego is involved in your addictions:

- **By Fueling Dissatisfaction:**

The ego cannot survive if you are feeling peaceful and satisfied, so it seeks to find ways to make you feel out of balance, making you believe that you are constantly needing or wanting something extra. This is what keeps us always going back for that extra coffee, cigarette, slice of pie, or status update.

- **By Always "Needing" More:**

Enough is never enough for the ego. It will keep you under its rule by making you believe that you need more of this or more of that to be truly happy. It tells you that once you reach a certain point; that promotion, this Friday, or getting a girlfriend, for example, you will be truly happy. But once you reach those places, you are still dissatisfied. This is because the ego can never be satisfied, it's not in the nature of the ego.

- **By Making you Feel Inadequate:**

The only reason we get addicted to things is because we feel incomplete without them. There is something "wrong" with us that can only be fixed by indulging in that addictive impulse, whether it be alcohol or obsessive social media use.

- **By Keeping you in Unhealthy Situations:**

When you are strong in yourself and peaceful, the ego cannot thrive or take over. This is why it keeps us dependent on negative emotions, stimulants, and even bad relationships. Relationships are also very addictive, even when they are unhealthy, and this keeps us in a weakened state where the ego can take over and run our lives.

How to Break the Ego Pattern of Addictive Behavior:

The good news is that even if you're addicted to something like most people are, you don't have to continue to succumb to those urges of the ego. Here are some tips for breaking the pattern of addiction:

- **Wait instead of Immediately Indulging:**

Next time you feel the urge to pick up your smart phone to check Facebook again, or to keep going back for more cake even though you are already full, do yourself a favor, and pause. Pay attention to the impulse as it keeps popping up, taking this opportunity to notice the patterns of your ego and the lies it tries to tell you.

- **search the Psychology of Addiction:**

If you read more into how addiction works, it will be easy to notice that it is completely based in ego and insecurity. Becoming more aware of the complexity behind this relationship will give you the ability to look beyond it and become stronger.

- **Replace Bad Habits with Good Ones:**

The best way to quit an unhealthy behavior is to replace it with a better one. If you have a habit of being in bad relationships over and over, try joining a club in your town instead. If you are a smoker, go for a run every time you crave a smoke. If you drink soda, start replacing it with water, or decide that instead of checking your social media updates constantly, you will do something productive every time the urge strikes.

This will put your own personal power back where it belongs, your hands. By being strong enough to make conscious choices about how you spend your time, you will become a better person who is less ruled by the ego.

Chapter 8: How being Present Helps

The ego is mostly centered on constantly being dissatisfied with reality. Wherever you are, and however you are, is never enough to satisfy the ego. This means that it constantly needs to remember the past and project into the future, comparing the present and constantly pointing out ways in which it fall short. This is an illusion that is meant to keep the ego alive and thriving, to keep you under its control.

You can start to take this power back by deciding to always be present for your life. This means resisting the urge to want to be somewhere else and accepting where you are right now, in this moment.

Here are some Tips for Being More Present:

- **Pay Attention to your Breathing:**

The breath is always there and can serve as an anchor to bring us back to a calm, present state of being. Next time you notice that you're getting caught up in the antics of the ego or getting upset over something, pause, and notice your stream of breath flowing in and out. You can inhale on three counts, then exhale on three counts, or even hold your breath for a second or two in between.

It's up to you to find which method works best. It's not a matter of following along strict instructions, but about creating your own way of doing things. Eventually, you will have your own reliable method for watching your breathing.

- **Write Down your Dreams:**

Dreams can be a valuable source of insight into our subconscious minds and fears. Some people believe that they "don't dream" since they hardly remember them, but everyone dreams. To start remembering yours, you only need to start writing them down each morning. This will teach you a lot about your own self and the nature of your ego, making clear things that were confusing before.

- **Notice the Beauty in Small Things:**

The essence of present-ness is noticing the beauty of the world. When we take a look at an animal, a sunset, or a flower, we see that it exists in a calm state of being and doesn't worry or get caught up in mental antics. We can learn valuable lessons from these elements of nature by noticing this calm beauty and letting it touch us.

- **Sit Quietly instead of Distracting Yourself:**

We have trained ourselves to always need stimulation, but what if that is not a healthy way to live? Next time you want to switch on the TV or do something else to entertain yourself, try resisting that urge and instead, sitting quietly in a room alone. You will notice a lot of resistance from your ego, but keep still. This is a great way to notice the ways that your ego jerks you around and get stronger at resisting it and making your own decisions about what to focus on.

All in all, present-ness is the best way to detach from your ego. When you are in a still state of accepting reality, your ego has no power over anything. It is silenced by your own calm state of mind. This is how you come to own your own mind again instead of being tossed about by the whims of your ego.

If you follow the guidelines of this book, you will soon live a completely free and inspired life, full of healthy relationships, successful jobs, and most importantly, happiness.

Conclusion

Thank you again for downloading this book!

I hope this book was able to help you to learn about exactly what the ego is, notice the ways that it runs your life, and give you the inspiration to regain control over your existence. Nearly everyone is controlled by their ego in today's world, but not many of them notice it. Don't be one of these people who isn't aware of their own minds and always plays the victim. Once you become aware of the ego's patterns in your own life, you will start noticing it in all the people around you.

You can be an example to them by getting the reigns back over your own mind and being a shining source of inspiration. Instead of lecturing others about the ego, be sure to live freely. That is how you have the most influence over others.

The next step is to pay attention to the principals I outlined in this book and start improving yourself, today. You can take back control over your own life and mind and start living an existence that is free from turmoil and resistance.

Finally, if you enjoyed this book, then I'd like to ask you for a favor, would you be kind enough to leave a review for this book on Amazon? It'd be greatly appreciated!

Thank you and good luck!

About the Author

Fred Mercado is the president of <u>Mercado Consulting</u>; A Consulting company with a focus in the Enterprise and Wireless industry in North America and the Caribbean and Latin America - CALA. He holds an AS Degree in Avionics from Embry-Riddle Aeronautical University, a Bachelor of Science Degree in Business from Excelsior College of New York, and MBA in International Business from American Intercontinental University of Chicago.

Fred is an experienced business executive with over 30 years of professionalism in the business and telecommunication industry. He is a well-known leader and achiever as his expertise expands through domestic and international markets. He has worked in various executive level positions with several well established organizations including his time with Wireless Facilities Inc., Crown-Castle International, MetroPCS, and at McCaw Cellular Communications/AT&T Wireless. Fred also serves as a Board Advisor and technical & business consultant to several companies in the telecommunications industry.

Fred also has several internationally recognized certificates including Project Management Professional (PMP), Corporate Governance (Sarbanes Oxley - SOX) from Tulane University, Negotiations, and Organisational Behaviour, from Heriot-Watt University in the UK and is a certified Total Quality Management (TQM) Instructor. He has written several industrial papers that gained the attention of many and as an author writing a series of books to share his experience, knowledge and expertise in a bid to further educate, assist and build new leaders. His series covers every aspect in establishing knowledge and expertise in the field of Business, Project Management, and overall Leadership.

You can learn more about Fred by visiting:

www.mercadoconsulting.com

www.fredmercado.com

https://www.linkedin.com/in/fredmercado

Also visit my website at www.thenewleaders.com to join the team of leaders making a difference in today's society.

Bonus:

Subscribe to The New Leaders and receive a free eBook on Leadership.

Visit my site at www.thenewleaders.com and join my email list. When you sign up I will send you updates on advancements, news, educational information, and opportunities to help advance your leadership ambitions and skills.

I also have a Free eBook that I will send you upon joining the list. The ebook is full of relevant and extremely useful information on becoming a great leader, and a great source of information to home the leadership skills you already have.

It is free with no strings attached, just my way of thanking you for purchasing my book and joining the league of today influential leaders.

Printed in Great Britain
by Amazon